Menopause
A Hot Topic

… to Connie, Anna, Lily and Sarah
for when change comes

First Published by Parks Publications, London UK in 2019

Sam Bunch © 2019

A CIP catalogue for this book is available
from the British Library.

ISBN 978-1-9998804-1-5

Printed and bound in the UK

Graphic Design and front cover by Alison Gardner
Artwork by Charlotte Hardy

Also available by the author

Follow me at collectingconversations.com

Hot Topics

The credible contributor…

We are all experts on our own menopause that's for sure but it's always good to find someone who has gone the extra mile. Hilary Baxter is one such woman. She really has done her research. She's got herself a PhD on the subject!

A few months ago I was telling my hairdresser I was writing a book on the menopause. 'You won't believe it' she said, 'a client of mine is doing her PhD on the menopause - you have to get in touch with her'. I love serendipity. I rang Hilary immediately and asked her what she was up to. She explained that her research was based on interviewing women about their menopause and then incorporating what she found into an art installation. She sounded like a woman on a mission, and I wanted to meet her. A few weeks later we met up; drank tea, ate cake and chatted about the dastardly subject. I asked her if she would write a few words for my book. She said 'YES'.…

Foreword

TODAY, as every day, thousands of women across the world will have their menopause. Some will not even realise they have had it, others will have gone through a wide range of physical indicators, sometimes for as long as ten years before. All women will go through menopause if they live long enough, and yet, up until this decade, relatively little has been shared about the experience in the public domain. The menopause is a physical stage of female life; it is not an illness. The terminology has been unattractively medicalised by terms such as 'vaginal atrophy' with offers of replacing hormones with one substance or another and a plentiful supply of lubricants. The research on the effect of the menopause is woefully patchy for something that more than fifty per cent of the population will go through during their long lives.

The current generation of menopausal women have been astonished to find that previously lived experiences of the menopause have been reduced to sporadic advice from medical professionals and endless Google searches for information and solutions. These women are searching for anything that might provide an explanation or even short-term relief, even as they experience a gradual but perceptible erasure from public life. It has seemed at times as if menopause is a new thing and that no-one else has ever dealt with its side-effects until very recently. A thick fog of silence has descended so completely that even mother to daughter conversations on personal experiences seem to have rarely taken place. But over the past year there has been a discernible shift, because conversations about the menopause are now being heard on the airwaves, on television, in print, in public meetings as well as in private. No subsequent generation of women needs to be uninformed about what menopause might mean to them. The conversations have been started.

Menopause is an individual experience for every woman; some will be like our own, some completely different, some will make us laugh out loud (a form of gallows humour) and others will make us groan or cry. But by sharing individual experiences honestly and expressing our thoughts and ideas we begin to make sense of the menopause for ourselves and for the next generation of women.

Hilary Baxter. PhD

Practice-based research on Scenography & Menopause.
London July 2019.

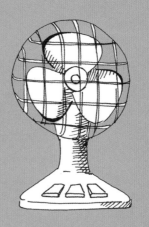

If you're looking for answers - I don't have any!

I'LL make it quick. My attention span has dwindled to the size of a gnat but there are things I need to get off my chest.

I never intended to write my musings on the menopause. I wasn't that interested. I'd heard about it, seen friends spontaneously combust right in front of my eyes for no apparent reason and, as for my own mum, well, she diarised 'the best bits' throughout her 10 year ordeal - but no, that wasn't going to happen to me. Deep sigh, it did.

It was just a couple of weeks ago after reaching the end of yet another tether that I decided to share my own highlights. I woke one morning, my brain bursting with ideas. I got out my laptop ready to purge my thoughts. All of a sudden a whoosh of apathy and blatant disregard for my

{ Hot Flushes }

creative enthusiasm washed over me. I couldn't be bothered. That's typical of the menopause: one minute you give a shit, the next you don't! In fact, 'I can't be arsed' and 'fuck it' seem to be my new attitude. I'm almost adolescent.

'You've changed' my friend tells me. Umm, I think she's right. I hope I don't feel like this for much longer because this hideousness is ruining my life. Once upon a time I was enthusiastic, passionate, a curious person, excited about life but as oestrogen rushes to find her nearest exit I find myself appearing to be a little indifferent about - well, almost everything!

So what to do about all this confusion and apathy? Not a lot it seems because just when I think everything in my life needs an overhaul including job, diet and husband, it all changes.

{ Irregular Periods}

I appreciate you might be thinking this woman is all over the place and somedays I am but please bear witness to my suffering for the sake of all the women who've gone before us. Those whose voices never got to share this kind of chat and for the ones who are coming up behind us. They need to know what's coming.

Honesty is key so I am not holding back. I want to be clear: the menopause is taking its toll and like most things I feel better when I share my pain.

I've been going through IT for three years now and whilst I'm melting most days there's no sign of it evaporating. So from me, a hormonally challenged woman please accept my menopausal offering. A small contribution, a keepsake, a homage to our ever-changing bodies.

I've asked a few other menopausal women (52

{ Fatigue }

to be exact) for words of comfort - or discomfort, - on this complex topic. A thought, a paragraph, a quote on what they think. There's space for you to add your own commentary too, then when younger generations ask 'What is it like?' at least you'll have a record because let's face it - you won't remember.

I have included poetry too. I have no idea why but for some reason I've started doodling 'rhymes of passion'. When I wake in the night with some weird symptom or other, I grab my pen and jot down my daft thoughts. They're not exactly Carol Ann Duffy but they have provided me with a mildly amusing distraction. They make me laugh and squirm in equal measure.

{ Memory Lapses }

Once
Sweet lips
Slender hips

(I never had slender hips, it just rhymed)

Now
Cursed lips
Knackered hips

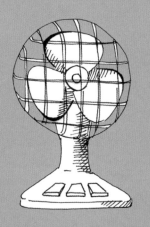

My body's deficient
so I'm told
My body's inefficient
so I'm told
My body's insufficient
so I'm told

You lack
I'm told
You're low
I'm told
You're old
I'm told

On a bad day I agree
on a good day - I'M ME!

SOME women have no symptoms. I'm told one fifth of women actually get away, scot free, – ABSOLUTELY NOTHING AT ALL! I wish you well but get out of my way with your good fortune - I have much to discuss.

I make no apologies that this is all about me. I'm a 51 year old, married, menopausal woman with children almost grown and life as I knew it is over - I need my space! Virginia Woolf wrote about the importance of 'A room of one's own' and if it's good enough for Virginia it's good enough for me. I've invested in one, a room that is - well, actually it's a shed at the bottom of my garden. You'll find me in there most days.

Let's get straight down to it: this menopause business has taken me a little by surprise. I knew it

{ Hot Flushes }

was coming but like anything you have to experience it to really know what it's like and I can tell you - I'm not keen.

The Perimenopause

The 'condition' you don't necessarily know you're in until you come out of it, then realise you were in it, because THAT was easy compared to what's coming next.

Five years ago some weird stuff started happening. A conveyor belt of surprises were being thrown at me, the prequel, a taster session of things to come, a welcome party. 'Come on in, try everything!'. I tried everything (well almost). New daily symptoms bombarded me. I had five weeks of hell!

{ Loss of Libido }

Searing ovulation pain like never before. Lax, loose muscles culminating in weekly trips to the physio. I'm confused: how can my body feel like jelly but at the same time feel incredibly tight and restricted? Everything hurts. Heat is steaming out of me. My face is permanently red and perhaps to the untrained eye might give the appearance that I am a healthy, long distant runner. This is misleading as I would never ever do such a thing.

There's weight gain. I'd unlikely get away with that one and frankly it's far too boring to dwell on - there's more novel symptoms grabbing my attention than that old chestnut! For example, the pain in my right shoulder blade that will not go away. Two years, it's been hanging around for! Then one day, without any explanation, it went away.

{ Vaginal Dryness }

I woke most nights - well you would do with that pain. Eventually drifting back to sleep only to be woken in the morning by intense heat whooshing through my entire body, a feeling that takes my breath away. I've taken to draping myself in a sheet of pure Egyptian cotton. I might as well adorn my inner goddess even if she is hot and sweaty.

My skin's so dry my lips stick together. There's indigestion and exhaustion. Intermittent hot flushes out of the blue and with no warning. Last week I went bright red after eating a chicken sandwich. All this would make for a very good comedy sketch if it weren't so fucking awful. It's a

{ Mood Swings }

bit alarming and this was just the start!

I read an article by the inimitable Jeanette Winterson about bioidentical hormones and a very expensive trip to The Marion Gluck Clinic. I booked in - ouch, £300 for an appointment. Their conclusion is I'm perimenopausal and, wait for it, I need testosterone! WHAT? I would have thought that was the last thing I needed.

I'm not one for taking stuff, mainly because I forget. I collect my prescription and go home to mull. The mulling took another two years. I didn't take anything. Things settled down. I had no idea this was the starter, the entrée, the beginning of my metamorphosis.

{ Panic attacks }

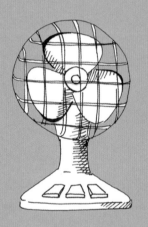

Flushed to a sweat
Like when we first met
A different kind of moan
A wailing hormone.

Flushed like a beetroot
Tired and hot
Pools of cool sweat
My cleavage, the lot.

THEN it started good and proper. May, three years ago - my periods just stopped and everything changed. As symptoms arose I jotted them down. Don't ask me why but I'm glad I did. I clearly have a deep desire to share my pain. So here goes - there's a list and it's long.

HAIR: initially falling out and thinning.
SKIN: legs itchy to the point I make them bleed, scratching - wakes me at up night.
FACE: RED RED RED
EYES: stabbing pain as though someone has poked a burning needle in the centre of my eye. The pain is something else. My eyelashes have literally let themselves go. Unbuckling out of their sockets like tiny parachutes, they float down my cheeks. There are gaps - will they grow back?

{ Hot Flushes }

MOUTH: last Christmas I developed fangs. After a Google search it seems I have Angular Cheilitis: 'Inflammation of one or both corners of the mouth, often the corners are red with skin breakdown and crusting'. I actually have breakdown and crusting!

TEETH: gum recession. I think that might just be the ageing process but I do need to use a toothpick after every meal.

TONGUE: weirdly rough and sore. The surface of my tongue feels like sandpaper and things don't taste like they used to, although it's not stopping me eating!

NOSE: interesting scabs forming on the inside - I've resorted to nose picking!

EARS: are fine, phew!

NECK: morphing slowly into a turkey.

SHOULDERS: oh the pain, the pain. Knots the size of melons, as are my boobs.

{ Urinary Tract Infection }

BOOBS: thankfully pain free but enormous. Increase in cup size again and I've got nipple chafe (just to reiterate, no running took place during the making of my menopause).

NAILS: weak, brittle - a bit like my mood!

BACK: doesn't hurt unless I exercise, so I'm not exercising.

ARMS: achy, achy achy and peculiar lumps have formed. No idea what's going on but I am sick of going to the doctors so I'm not going to find out.

RIBS: they don't hurt until touched then I'm through the roof in pain. It's my muscles, apparently - they are weak. 'Exercise' they say. 'Fuck off' I say. I've never been so rude!

STOMACH: indigestion, gurgling, tightness, my stomach feels like it's moved and is sitting on my diaphragm which is awkward as I can't breathe!

{ Bloating }

TUMMY: a flat tyre would be preferable to the fat tyre I've got. The bathroom scales reveal yet another stone on. JOY! I'm so heavy it's comical; clinically obese according to my BMI. I think it's a height restriction myself and nothing that a bit of baggy linen won't hide. Do I have attitude, apathy or acceptance? I cant decide!

DIAPHRAGM: can't get enough breath. Feels like I need a jump start. I'm not firing on all cylinders.

HEART: weird pains - is it anxiety, panic or am I having a heart attack?

BUM: I am now wearing EXTRA big knickers to keep it all tucked in. There's nothing worse than a middle aged woman scooping her knickers out of her bum en route to the bus stop.

HIPS: I can't, I really can't go into it. I would bore you off this page. Let's just say there's pain, moaning and agony on repeat. And the physio is on speed dial.

{ Hair Loss }

THIGHS: I used to be a gymnast, not a very good one but I could do back flips and the splits, so naturally I was quite good at yoga. Back in my 20s I used to go just to show off! Not anymore. All inversions cause gravity to push my tummy fat on to my boobs which pushes my chin, mouth and nose into a mushy suffocating mess. The whole humiliating descent causes mild panic and claustrophobia. Oh how life teaches you humility. I can still touch my toes but have to reach over the mountain of fat in my middle and it hurts. It hurts so much I went to the doctors. 'Am I fat or is there something hideous growing inside me?'. It transpires I'm just fat and she's clearly concerned as a few months later I get a random call - 'You have an appointment at our 'Change for Life Group'. I genuinely thought they'd got the wrong

{ Sleep Disorders }

number. You see unlike most women, I think I'm thinner than I am. Some might say delusional - I say my glass is always full! I'm now signed up to a 'Fat Club'. This will get me sorted!

'Fat Club' didn't get me sorted because I like cake - a lot. Cake is and always has been life's great saviour. It isn't Jesus: everyone knows it's cake that really gets to the heart of the matter!

Where was I? Oh yes -

MY ACHILLES HEEL: getting out of bed in the morning I stagger to the loo. This symptom has hung around the longest so far. It's really painful. I eventually call the doctors - again. She tells me it's Achilles tendonitis after a bout of Plantar Fasciitis - it's all sounding a little inflammatory! Apparently another menopausal delight. I now have a permanent hobble.

{ Dizziness }

BOWELS: wind and constipation. But then at least I'm not pooing my pants as some women I've spoken to are….!

BELLY: the fat is on a roll!

VAGINA: can't disclose. I have a teenage son. The trauma for him would be worse than my explanation. Use your imagination. You've read stuff, you know what's happening.

TOE NAILS: fungal infection and discolouration.

BONES: thankfully not brittle but very achy.

FEET: I have actually gone up a whole shoe size but it doesn't matter. I took to wearing Birkenstocks a long time ago.

MEMORY: FOG. Life is becoming very unclear.

HAIR & SKIN: after the initial bout of thinning I got supersized growth. My hair has become

{ Weight Gain }

uncannily thick and very, very soft. I know, I know, this isn't something you should complain about. People spend a fortune trying to get their hair and skin silky soft but for the first time since I can remember I don't need hair conditioner and the tips of my fingers are softer than a new born baby's. I can't see my fingerprints, they've been smoothed out. It's disconcerting. I do yet another Google search - 'What does it mean if you have VERY soft skin?'. 'A gene mutation' they say, and 'people with it have excessive stretching of their skin and joints' - Hurrah! I am Mrs Incredible after all.

GENERAL DEMEANOUR: absolutely knackered. Once I could spend an entire day gardening. I'll be lucky if I can lift the lawn mower out of the shed these days, I have no muscle strength.

BODY ODOUR: I'm a bit smelly.

{ Incontinence }

THESE symptoms are boring but need airing. Stuff is happening. I have friends who think they're depressed and their self-esteem is lower than the Mariana Trench!

Women use to get locked up or had frontal lobotomies back in the day and it's no wonder, this menopause business is verging on insanity.

Two years after my first trip I'm back at The Marion Gluck Clinic. Cheaper for the follow-up but only just! Blood tests reveal I am now a fully dysfunctioning menopausal woman. There's stuff to take: Vitamin D, maybe some oestrogen gel, definitely some DHEA (never heard of it but apparently it's the 'fun' hormone). I could do with some fun because after a follow-up with my doctor (to compare results), I am told 'Yes you're in the menopause. Don't have sugar, coffee or alcohol,

{ Headaches }

you'll be more tired, your skin will dry out and your sex drive is likely to be zero (no change there then!). Eat lots of fruit and veg and exercise as much as you can'. Fun you say?

I've moaned a lot during my menopause. In fact I have three journals full of symptoms, self-analysis and lists of stuff that I 'should' be doing to improve my life, my body and my sanity. It's confusing. For instance, should I be taking…

Agnus Castus? Magnesium? Calcium? Black Cohosh? Omega 3, 6 or 9 for that matter? Zinc? Starflower oil? Vitamin D? Acidophilus? Flax? Protein? Soya? Iron? Sage? The list goes on and on and there are no rules. Then there's all the hormones; Testosterone? DHEA? Anti-depressants? Progesterone cream? Oestrogen gel?

There's advice, information, should's, could's,

{ Burning Tongue }

would's. It's too much. I'm losing the will to get out of bed… incidentally, did you ever read that book *'The woman who went to bed for a year?'*. I can see the appeal.

Occasionally I think 'Right, I'm done, HRT it is then'. But as soon as I get the prescription everything stops and a tiny bit of the old me returns.

In all honesty my symptoms come and go and it's hard to keep track of what's what. I'm now a regular at the doctors. At first she prescribed anti-depressants - not because I'm depressed but apparently they help with unusual aches. Are you fucking kidding me. Every part of my body is aching - there's nothing unusual about it. It's constant! (I still don't take the drugs).

Confession. I've taken to wearing compression socks. They make me feel supported. I think that's

{ Digestive Problems }

half the battle. I don't feel supported - not because I don't have friends but because society doesn't do menopausal women. In fact, society doesn't do anyone over 45 if we're honest. But hey back to me - remember it's all about me.

I've had a lot of symptoms but by no means all of them, although the fogginess in my brain seems to have upped it's game recently. I've developed pain in my left shoulder now too and there's a general vagueness about me. It's a miracle that I am still able to put this book together. Most days I say 'I can't remember' at least 20 times. I come home at night (from my shed) and my husband asks how my day was. I give him a vacant look as we settle down to watch some kind of box set. This I must tell you takes us 10 - 15 minutes of flicking through the channels. What was it we were

{ Muscle Tension }

watching last night? Was it on catch-up, recorded, Netflix, Amazon or iPlayer? Was it a crime drama? A comedy? It's ludicrous. Maybe the menopause memory loss is affecting him too. All I can say is thank God I'm not a brain surgeon or pilot, or someone who actually requires a serious amount of concentration for their job.

There are many, many more symptoms that I have not yet had the pleasure of. Hopefully I won't, but I hear tears are common and not the ones of joy! There's frustration, exhaustion, confusion, and migraines. Hair growth - and not in the usual places, then just when you think your periods have gone for good you're caught off guard. Not a sanitary towel to be found. You stopped buying them months ago and well, it's all very messy.

{ Allergies }

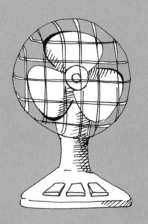

Evolving pains

Weight gains

Scarlet cheeks

Embarrassing leaks

Indecent assaults

Hair moults

Night sweats

Memory forgets

MY conclusion is - I don't like the menopause. I find it all too much. It's changed me - and not for the better. I've slowed right down (perhaps not a bad thing) and I sleep a lot. I find myself wanting to nap around 11am and then again at 3pm! My energy has drifted into the abyss. Recently and perhaps most worryingly, I made lunch; ate it, forgotten I'd eaten it. Made a second one, then ate that. Only realising when I saw my first plate in the dishwasher. This is madness!

I've decided to check out one of the menopause clinics set up by the NHS because for all my 'suck it and see' attitude I am knackered, fed up and ready to move on from this.

I got a referral letter which tells me I might have to wait! Apparently the waiting list is full so I am now waiting to get onto the waiting list.

{ Acne }

And as for HRT, there are rumours about an impending national shortage. Clearly there's a demand for advice, help and support but I'm not sure there's enough to go around.

Last week when I was feeling more upbeat I re-read something about the menopause that I first read 30 years ago. I made a note to myself at the time 'keep this - it will be useful when this happens to me'. It went something along the lines of menopause being a transformation, women coming out of the cocoons of convention, restriction, roles, and life stages. Having been moulded partly by society and partly by biology. Those structures are morphing into something else. We are breaking down our shells. It's hard, exhausting and sweaty work. Scary, unpredictable and challenging. But once we've broken though we

{ Alopecia }

become free, wise women - the finest versions of ourselves. (I'm clinging to this idea, and it better be right!).

Menopause is constantly changing. There's no getting away from it, some women have an awful, awful time, others manage but it's not a bed of roses and there are a few fortunate souls that escape the drama. But there's always hope that there is in fact life at the end of this dark, frumpy, grumpy tunnel but it's trying to remain sane until then.

A final thought from Julian of Norwich (who?) - a 14th century female hermit who after a vision from the Virgin Mary wrote 'All shall be well, and all manner of things shall be well'. I for one am counting on it.

{ Brittle Nails }

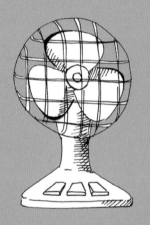

Sadly when I find myself
in times of trouble
Mother Mary doesn't
come along speaking
words of wisdom to me,
I have to hunt it out and
fortunately I've found
it in bucket loads.

THE favourite part of my job is researching and interviewing people. I love it for many reasons but the main one is learning that you're not alone. Listening to people is sometimes all the reassurance you need.

The following are comments from over 50 women I've spoken with who are either about to enter the menopause, are in it, or have come out the other side of it!

{ Hot Flushes }

" The menopause throws you straight back into all that uncertainty and insecurity of puberty but, because of prevailing societal attitudes, without the hope and promise. This is where the fundamental change is necessary. We must see the hope and promise from this stage of our lives, ourselves. Change our attitude one menopausal woman at at time and I think the word 'patriarchy' should be in this quote along with 'fucking' and 'shitty!'." **Nikki 54**

" ME - No - PAUSE! That's the problem we don't pause. Pause! Pause! Pause! It will pass - everything does'." **June 56**

{ Body Odour }

" I have often heard it said that men blame their divorces on their wife's menopause. This happened to me. He was told to hang on in there, she will come right and return to her senses eventually. 'It's just her hormones', meanwhile I was thinking clearly for the first time in years. It's quite comical that the man can't take any responsibility for a situation so he blames it on his wife's menopause!" **Amy 48**

" The hot flushes are the worst. The bedsheets come off then go back on again. I'm constantly telling my husband to 'get away, get away'. I'm too hot! The broken sleep does my head in." **Karen 57**

{ Itchy Skin }

> " I've got used to that fact that I can burst in to flames of sweat at any given moment. My moods really do swing. If I am honest I was determined for my menopause to be the making of me and I think it has been. I listen to my body more. I'm more gentle with myself and that's got to be a benefit. A new thing I've just started doing; whenever I get really hot and I'm in the house, providing it's just the two of us, I just strip off. Even to the point of taking my bra off and resting my boobs on the cool surface of the kitchen table while we eat - he's happy, I'm happy. It's a win win situation."

Fayon 50

{ Osteoporosis }

" Raised on the roll-up-your-sleeves-and-get-on-with-it approach, I tend not to dwell... Having said that, mushy brain is a thing. Random absorbing waves of inner radiation are a thing. Nipping into the garage for a ....nope, sorry, no idea what I came in for... is definitely a thing.

A solitary tampon, somewhat forlorn, reminiscing over our mutual menstrual shenanigans. Her sole bedfellow an equally redundant pink foam toe separator, nestled in at the bottom of my junk drawer. I should really think about decluttering ... if only I were able ...to think." **Rachel 51**

" I'd just like to feel like the old me, all of the time." **Jess 50**

{ Tingling Skin }

" The word 'Change' means just that. It's not just our change, it's everyone's change. We need to change our attitudes, assumptions and judgements about middle-aged women and the menopause. Women are at the forefront of change which tells me it's a good thing." **Jayne 51**

" Sometimes I wake up in the morning and I hate my whole family. I know it's me and not them but I don't give a flying fuck. I don't have any philosophy about this. I just say what I think and obviously I'm always right. My patience and tolerance is being really tested." **Caron 51**

{ Insomnia}

" I've lost a bit of control over my faculties, I wear a panty liner everyday in case a little bit of wee comes out." **Elaine 51**

" I think I've been lucky. I haven't really noticed the menopause. Nine years ago I had breast cancer followed by chemotherapy and went straight onto Tamoxifen. I went into a forced menopause because Tamoxifen blocks oestrogen. I've had night sweats and achy joints on and off ever since but I put these symptoms down to having the drugs rather than the menopause. So I don't actually know if I've had the menopause. I feel so much better now." **Jackie 54**

{ Difficulty Concentrating }

" The menopause ages you on all levels. I feel like a dried out wrinkled old prune. I'm embarrassed by the flushes. It's totally humiliating that people can see you going through the ageing process. I feel much more invisible than I used to." **Julie 55**

" I have revengeful fantasies about the colleague at work who can sneeze and just carry on with whatever she was doing! There are days too when I can eat my way through the entire contents of my fridge, still be hungry. Contemplate a Gin & Tonic before remembering I am a fully paid up member of Slimming World!" **Sam 48**

{ Irregular Heartbeat }

" My behaviour is erratic. I have cluster migraines. I am more emotional and tearful about things than I ever used to be. No one told me what was happening then a woman from work said, 'Right, this is what it is - it's the menopause'. I began to talk about it more openly. There's HRT but I don't want to take it. I want to go through my menopause intensely, to feel what it's like to be this emotional. I was one of those people that thought emotions didn't have a place at work. I wasn't an emotional person and had little tolerance for it in other people. I am much more tolerant now. The menopause isn't a disability but adjustments need to be made. It's about

{ Anxiety }

support. Statistics speak for themselves. Women have to work longer therefore the menopause needs addressing. Our behaviour can be challenging. It needs to be normalised just as you do with mental health issues. I've set up a menopause policy at work and they have agreed to do menopause training. The menopause is just part and parcel of who you are so embrace it." **Marie 52**

As far as I can tell I am still in the early stages of perimenopause. My periods are regular, just a bit heavier than before. Some vaginal dryness, but lube during sex sorts that, no discomfort." **Rachel 53**

{ Depression }

" The worst point for me has been the mood changes. Feeling totally and utterly overwhelmed by sudden changes in emotions. A wave of anxiety or sadness would come crashing over me. It would only last for a day or two but long enough to unsettle me and everyone else in the house. I thought I was depressed. I spent one weekend lying on the kitchen bench weeping, not even crying. It was frightening. I was utterly out of control of my own emotions. I felt I was changing into someone I really didn't like.

I think the kids and my husband thought I was losing it, that weekend he took the boys out of the situation, was that right thing for me? Possibly not. I would have

{ Breast Pain }

like them to sit with me, to bear witness. You feel alien enough in your own body. So to have them be with me would have been better. I haven't hidden anything from the kids. They know everything; that I'm on HRT, that the hot sweats and my mood changes are all part of it. I don't know how I would have managed this without a supportive partner." **Lucie 52**

" I told my male friend that I was having a hot flush and he said 'it's just a flush' and I said there's no JUST about it. Unless you've experienced how uncomfortable and embarrassing they are you have absolutely no idea." **Lesley 56**

{ Joint pain }

" It's knowing that you're not alone. I can tell something has changed. I was talking to a friend and telling her I felt this fogginess. I felt dreadful, really low and really down. I've been prescribed oestrogen gel and I think it is helping but how much of it is psychosomatic? Saying that, the aches are not psychosomatic and the PMT blues have definitely got worse, albeit for just a few days a month but it ain't nice. All we really want to know is what are we are actually dealing with?" **Maria 52**

" There's a lot of taking your cardigan on and off. Apparently it could go on for another 20 years." **Flick 59**

{ Nose bleeds }

" Mood Swings. Empowering. Nausea-ting. Overpowering. Palpitations. Age Spots. Unusually Hot. Still sexy. Earthy. Engaging." **Gill 64**

" As soon as you start speaking to other women going though the menopause you realise you're not going mad. There is a huge benefit to feeling part of a community especially of people going through the same thing. We have to support each other - there's no hierarchy of suffering, it's shit for almost everyone going through it. I'm not sure you can get through the menopause without humour. The whole thing is terrifying." **Terri 53**

{ Night Sweats }

66 The single simplest piece of advice I can give to anyone entering the menopause is probably the hardest one to accept socially: after years of enjoying the social lubrication of alcohol if you want to minimise the consequences that go with the menopause, it is best to stop the booze straight away! You sleep better, wake up less tired, therefore eat less, have fewer hot sweats and overall feel absolutely bloody amazing - I still can't believe the clarity that not drinking gives you. Drinking today is a conspiracy by the industry to just keep you addicted. Break the habit and find a new you!"
Deborah 53

{ Tightness in chest }

" Today I've had 22 hot flushes. The worst of it is the head rush I get that comes with them. I feel my head is going to explode. My body becomes so hot. If I could take off all my clothes wherever I am, I would. I sweat so much I put deodorant under my tits. I'm always complaining that I'm too hot. I must drive my friends and family mad. I've noticed I've started grinding my teeth, clenching them, biting down trying to stop the heat rising in me. I feel angry, clumsy and aggressive at times. I can't wait for all this to end. I can't talk to you anymore, I'm off to sit in a cold bath." **Carole 53**

{ Finger nail ridges }

❝ It was August, six years ago. Suddenly a flush came over me from nowhere. I was the colour of a tomato and there was nowhere to hide. For the next five months there were fans on permanently in every room in the house, even in midwinter. I felt as though I had been put in an oven. My face was perpetually red. I lost my confidence, I lost my ability to do simple things. I loved cooking but I couldn't even get my act together to decide which recipe to choose. Literally I would be sat on the sofa for hours at a time and achieve absolutely nothing. I used to go to the gym. I'd arrive at the car park but couldn't muster the enthusiasm to get myself into the class

{ Eye problems }

(and my coordination was all over the place too) so I'd drive home again. It wasn't like me. I consider myself to be a cheerful, optimistic person.

Eventually I went to the doctors. The tears poured out of me. He asked if I wanted to take anti depressants as they would help with the redness and my mood. I didn't think I was depressed but I took them anyway, just a small dose. Within a week the redness disappeared and a few weeks later my body adjusted to them. I think the tablets helped me build my confidence back up again. A few months later I forgot to take a pill and my symptoms seemed ok so I didn't take one the following day, then the day after too. Then I just stopped altogether. Later my

{ Aches... }

doctor told me that it wasn't a good idea just to stop but I did what I felt was right. My menopause was thankfully short-lived, five months in total, but they were intense days. Loss of confidence, terrible hot sweats, a red flushed face and no drive whatsoever." **Alex 56**

" I seem to spend a lot of time asking other people if they're hot - or is it just me, although it's the summer but I think it's mostly me? ... and another thing I thought I'd hurt my ankles from running so I stopped but it seems aching ankles in the morning is just another symptom... guess I should start running again...!" **Alison 52**

{ ...and pains }

" Why do we Western women have such difficulty with the meno-pause when Eastern women seem to embrace this chapter of their lives. The younger generations in the East see women as older and wiser. They gain respect as they age and therefore age gracefully. We Westerners seem to fight it which is maybe one of the reasons our symptoms create havoc with our bodies." **Sally 53**

" My hair started falling out a lot. I think I've got alopecia. There are bald patches appearing. I feel bad enough as it is but this is just making things worse. If it carries on I'll be bald soon. Talk about losing your femininity." **Tina 56**

{ Migraines }

" I seem to have become an overly anxious person and I don't recognise myself as it doesn't seem like the real me. I'll stress unnecessarily about day-to-day things going wrong - so every train is going to be missed, every bit of equipment in the house is on the verge of malfunctioning, every arrangement will be a disaster, every ache is something serious. It causes sleepless nights and feels like such a negative and draining way to be. It's called something like 'catastrophe anxiety' and it's driving me and my family a bit mad.

I really hope it will pass. I'd like to go back to being the laid-back person I feel like I used to be." **Elizabeth 57**

{ Loss of confidence }

" I remember one morning when I was walking to work; it was freezing, ice on pavement, cutting wind, drizzle and despite my winter warm coat and hat I was still freezing. (I've always felt the cold, even when others have shorts and t-shirts on) Suddenly I felt a hot flush starting. I got warmer and warmer. It was great. It was just like an internal radiator and it kept me warm till I reached the office. But it never happened like that again. However every time I felt the cold after that I recalled the day. I felt as if my body was on my side for a change instead of going off and doing its own thing." **Julie 58**

{ Moaning }

" It feels a bit like when you were about to start your periods all those years ago. You're quite excited. There's an element of me that's embracing a change in my life. It doesn't mean you're going down-hill. I feel more confident and it's quite exciting." **Hannah 53**

" When I was 49 my periods suddenly got very claggy and erratic. My body became very stiff. I was still very interested in sex but I felt less attractive. I felt my husband thought I was less attractive too and I was right - he left me for the classic younger woman when I was 54. My periods stopped altogether after that." **Geraldine 60**

{ Hot Flushes }

" My first hot flush was when I was driving on the A3 towards Guildford. My arm resting on the open window frame and the sun's heat hit my arm. I felt a corresponding heat in the middle of my back- very sudden and hot. It went away again as quickly as it came. "A hot flush" I thought, "not so bad, OK, I can deal with that" - but I was very, very wrong." **Hilary 56**

" It's not you, it's IT! So don't think you're dying or going mad!" **Linda 54**

" I am literally fed up to the back teeth of feeling this way. Some days I think I'm losing my mind. I just want the old me back." **Sharon 49**

{ Heaviness }

" The menopause started showing up for me in my early 40s with my periods becoming even more irregular than ever. My last period was at age 48. I lived without too many symptoms for a few years and then things changed dramatically. Almost overnight I found I could not make a decision about anything, including work. I had been working at the same job for a couple of years and I knew it like the back of my hand but suddenly I started to question myself about every little detail. It was horrible. I didn't know what was wrong with me. This went on for a couple of weeks until I realised it was the menopause.

{ Fluid retention }

I knew I didn't want to take HRT so I read up about herbs. It was confusing as there were so many different ones to choose from. Some were general, others for more specific symptoms. I listed the pros and cons and ended up in a big knot. Eventually I went to see a herbalist and we decided on two herbs, one general and one specifically aimed at the lack of confidence. I started taking them and my confidence improved almost as fast as it had disappeared but, sadly, it's never gone back to where it was pre menopause.

I think this was some kind of signpost for me. I needed to make changes in my working life. The type of work I was doing became much less important to me.

{ Tendonitis }

I continued with the herbs for some years as well as taking progesterone cream but eventually my woolly-headedness became worse and I got myself into a mess trying to overanalyse things, wondering if I should be trying something else. In the end I couldn't stand it anymore - all the menopause cakes, the cold nettle tea, the seeds - I didn't have time to deal with it. I just stopped all of it and my head cleared. I think it was time anyway to stop the herbs. My body was ready to take over again. It's important to listen to your body because no matter how much you read and what supplements you take, your own body aways knows what's best for you. The hot flushes gradually went when I was 55. It was a relief." **Elaine 63**

{ Low self-esteem }

" I have nothing good to say about the menopause which started when I was 43. I still have hot flushes at 73, nobody can tell me why! Initially it started with such severe hot flushes, frequently night and day. It was a form of hideous torture and certainly wrecked my sleep pattern. They're not so severe now. The only benefit may be that it has aged me and thereby made me face my mortality - and that is probably the whole point of it from "Nature's" point of view. We are not meant to live forever, not even women!" **Heather 73**

" Hot sore nipples, feel cranky and tearful. My eyes are very dry and sore." **Tricia 53**

{ Lack of confidence }

66 Leave me alone, I'm changing."
Chris 50

66 I feel so sorry for my husband as he has a lot to contend with. I'm hot, I'm cold, I have palpitations and I've got headaches. I don't ever sleep through the night unless I'm drunk. There is a lot said about the menopause nowadays and we are lucky compared to our parents generation. At least we can talk about it without the fear of being ridiculed.

For me the worse bit so far is getting hairs on my chin and I have a nice moustache forming! I'm constantly plucking them out." **Amanda 53**

{ Exhaustion }

❝ I think the menopause defines you. I started mine at 46, which is quite young. I was working in a market research company with mainly young people. I would be in a meeting and have a hot flush. I could tell they thought I was embarrassed or stressed. I knew I couldn't stay in that environment. You're just not seen as credible.

I went on HRT. Life is too short and too manic to go through it naturally. The doctors put me on pills which gave me regular periods which was ironic as they had been erratic all my life.

Mentally I know I am super super moody and super super screamy. Physic-

{ Dry skin }

ally I've changed; my skin is more saggy. I used to be able to do a plank, all tight and firm, now my stomach just hangs on the floor. It's laughable.

I have been in a couple of new relationships and I can wake up in the night with the bed completely wet from sweating. What with that and the HRT dirty brown patches stuck on my bum, it's hardly sexy. There is a lot of pressure from society to do menopause naturally!" **Luby 48**

❝ Menopausal quips will be acceptable when we can all enjoy jokes about receding hairlines and balding." **Hilary 56**

{ Crying spells }

" The menopause broke me when I was already down. It left me, quite literally sobbing in the biscuit aisle of my local Tesco's with my bewildered sons in tow. I was deeply anxious, overwhelmed and desperate for a good night's sleep. Despite being 48 at the time, I simply didn't grasp it might be anything to do with my hormones. Six years on, what broke me has also helped heal me. I have learned to be kinder to myself. I've found joy in new things. I've taken up paddle-boarding which has opened up a lot of opportunities for me. I've joined the @2minutebeachclean campaign too. I collect plastic from local beaches and canals. I have created a new purpose for my future and have gratitude for my life." **Jo 54.**

{ Lack of motivation }

" I can't carry on like this, as it was. I want to change and to care less about what other people think. That's a big burden for a lot of women. My sensitivity has heightened and I'm feeling wobbly because I'm more vulnerable." **Gemma 51**

" I am not into HRT but my god I wouldn't have survived without it. I knew I had to do something when driving to a friends for supper I found myself steering towards a large brick wall! I left my car, got very drunk and spent the evening dancing around my friends kitchen. The next day I woke and thought fuck it, went straight to the doctors and got on HRT. It's truly worked for me." **Philippa 53**

{ Forgetfulness }

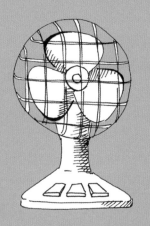

I haven't read anything or spoken to anyone who says the menopause is a 'good' experience. There are the optimists who think it's a wonderful transition and an opportunity for change but for the majority it's just about navigating the weeks, months and years until it's over. I think the most important thing is to know you're not alone and to find people to share your pain.

I've been in contact with The Menopause Café - set up by Rachel Weiss. The name got my attention on social media and I wanted to find out more. I asked her why she set up the Café...

66 I started The Menopause Café because I know that it is good to talk and create a community, to normalize and share information. To empower people to find their own solutions rather than relying on experts to tell them what to do. It's slower and more work to find your own path through your own menopause, but it's different for everyone and there is no one-size-fits-all solution or path or approach.

I am interested in the role of older women in our society. How we reorientate ourselves? Is menopause a wake-up call, to put ourselves first for a change, after decades of prioritizing our careers and families over our own bodily needs? Suddenly our bodies say "Stop, you need to listen to me! Now is the time to take care of me, feed me well, exercise me, be kind to me, honour my feelings". How do we take our place as wise women, with much to offer? How do we learn to slow down, whilst often also juggling caring for ageing parents, maintaining work performance, and sometimes also coping with teenagers?

These are the challenges we need to talk about. For the first time in decades I ask myself "What do I want now?" instead of "What do I have to do next?"

Once we break the silence and taboos,

then people will act. Whether that's to inform ourselves about coping strategies, to make opportunities for the third stage in life, or to campaign for menopause policies at work or in government, or education in schools and beyond. I don't have an agenda for what people should or shouldn't do, but I do want to enable conversations about menopause to take place so that men and women, young and old can feel free to speak about it if they wish to do so." **Rachel 53**

If you're interested in setting up your own café why not get in touch with Rachel, she can help you set up your own. www.menopausecafe.net*

BOOKS

I get overwhelmed with too much information but I found these books stopped me from going mad:

The Creative Menopause
by Farida Sharan

The Wisdom of the Menopause
by Christiana Northrup

Menopause - The Change for Better
by Henpicked

Hot Flushes, Cold Science: A History Of The Modern Menopause by Louise Foxcroft

Natural Solutions to Menopause
by Marilyn Glenville

SOCIAL MEDIA

There's so much information on social media but these sites sparked my interest:

The Menopause Collective - Instagram

Menohealthuk - Instagram

The Menopause Room - Facebook

The Menopause Café - twitter

Hotflushclub - Instagram

Menoandme - Instagram

PROFESSIONAL HELP

British Menopause Society at thebms.org.uk

Your own GP, get your bloods checked

NHS Menopause Clinics: they're not widespread but ask to be referred to your nearest.

The Marion Gluck Clinic, London at mariongluckclinic.com

Dr Louise Newson - The Menopause Doctor at menopausedoctor.co.uk

My Space…

My Space…

....

....

....

....

....

....

....

....

....

My Space…

....

....

....

....

....

....

....

....

....

....

....

....

....

....

....

....

....

....

....

....

Thank you

To all the women who've contributed their thoughts.
To Hilary for her foreword. Alison Gardner for her superb
design of the book and cover. Charlotte Hardy for her perfectly
formed illustrations, to Sian for proof reading and Sophie for
last minute corrections, and not forgetting Anthony the physio.

To the amazing people I've come across since entering the
world of writing and publishing who have supported my books
and projects. To friends, without which - what's the point?

And to YOU for buying my book.
I hope it brings a tiny bit of comfort.

You can find me on social media -
the usual suspects: Instagram, Twitter & FB

or my Blog collectingconversations.com. I try and post
regularly. Occasionally I forget, sometimes I'm not in the
mood and sometimes I just want to be left alone, so I don't!

A Last word -
Share your experiences, your wisdom, your insight, your
advice, and your kindness with other women. This sounds like
a no-brainer but as the First woman Secretary of State,
Madeleine Albright said -

There is a special place in hell for
women who don't help other women.